WISE MARIE SURVIVAL WORKBOOK

STREET-LEVEL GUIDE TO LIFE MASTERY

Written by Natasha Brune aka Kimberly Cano

WISE MARIE

SURVIVAL WORKBOOK

STREET-LEVEL GUIDE TO LIFE MASTERY

For those who don't come equipped with instincts—or
have lost them along the way.

NATASHA BRUNE

Connect with the Author
Join the adventure beyond the book! Stay updated on upcoming book tours, speaking events, and exclusive live webinars by invitation only. Sign up for the mailing list and be the first to know about special announcements.
📧 Email: InfoWiseMarie@gmail.com ● Website📧 TheWiseLadybug.com
Follow on Social Media: [@wiseladybug2025 Instagram | Kimberly Cano Kawaiola LinkedIn | The Wise Ladybug Facebook | The Triangle Mission
We have screenplays adapted from our stories, so please contact us if you wish to invest, collaborate, or otherwise in the film industry.
Additionally, I offer life and business coaching consulting services to help individuals and entrepreneurs align with their purpose, overcome obstacles, and achieve success. I tailor each program to the person and their needs.
Whether you resonate with Marie's journey or are seeking personal and professional growth, let's connect and explore opportunities to work together.

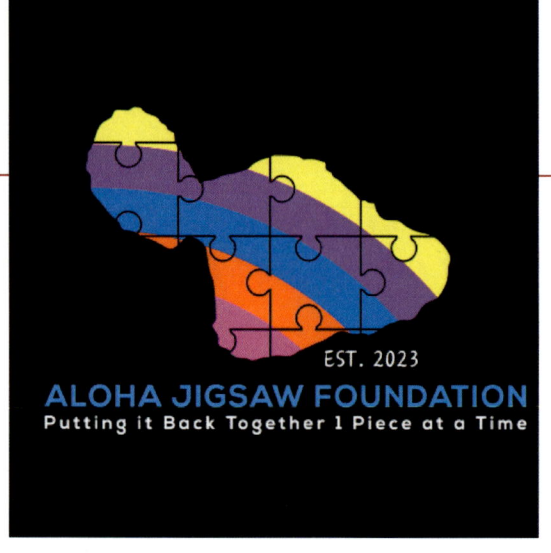

Supporting the Aloha Jigsaw Foundation

This book is dedicated to honoring the Aloha Jigsaw Foundation. A portion of the proceeds from Wise Marie and the Little Ladybug will go toward this effort, helping to create awareness and opportunities for children who see the world differently. One of our goals at the foundation is to commence the Spring 2026 Youth Trade and Mindset Academy on the Island of Maui, in honor of the children impacted by the 2023 Fires.

If this story resonates with you, I invite you to consider ADHD as a paradigm—an alternative way of viewing life, thinking creatively. And embracing unique perspectives. It is your superpower. We can multitask unlike any other human. Marie's journey is just the beginning. She is also the foundation for an adult series that challenges perceptions and paves the way for storytelling across multiple genres. As an author, my goal is to break boundaries and establish credibility in diverse literary spaces.

TABLE OF CONTENTS

CHAPTER ONE

INTRODUCTION

THE 11 YEAR ESCAPADE THAT TAUGHT ME EVERYTHING

Welcome to the truth. This workbook isn't for the polished. It's for the ones who've either lived on the edge—or are trying not to fall off it. In Wise Marie, you saw glimpses of my survival... Here's what I didn't say out loud: I became my own weapon, shield, GPS, therapist, and confidant. Now, I want you to become your own.

TRIGGER WARNING | DISCLAIMERS

This material is not meant to be therapy or a solution to what may be happening with you and your situation. Please use this as a guide, entertainment, or to learn what it is to be on the street and hustle for real. This is not for the faint-hearted or for critique. Take or leave the advice.

Data listed herein and in related materials may trigger drug abuse, mental, verbal, and physical abuse memories, PTSD of all types, bipolar episodes, and/or anxiety. If you are having thoughts of suicide or do not want to live, please seek help and call the suicide prevention line in your county.

The Author wishes to provide an insight into the world she lived in for 11 years, which spanned from the States of Hawaii, the Continental USA, and the Country of Japan. It was a different time then, with no or the infancy stages of technology. Today, it would be different because of this. Please keep this in mind when you are reading this workbook. The events occurred in the 70s, 80s, and 90s. Our team has done our best to keep it updated with current events and conveniences.

CHAPTER TWO

INSTINCT ACTIVATION - REBUILDING YOUR GUT COMPASS

JOURNAL PROMPT: WHEN DID I LAST IGNORE MY GUT, AND WHAT HAPPENED?

_____

_____

_____

_____

_____

_____

_____

_____

NOTES

....

....

....

....

....

....

....

....

....

....

....

MINI LESSON
INSTINCTS ARE INHERITED SURVIVAL CODES

Let's Build Them Back

Instincts are our body's original survival codes – deeply ingrained responses designed to keep us safe. These automatic reactions are built into our nervous system, shaped by evolution and reinforced by experience. When we encounter danger, stress, or uncertainty, our instincts activate to help us fight, flee, or adapt.

However, modern life often dulls these natural signals. Trauma, chronic stress, and constant overstimulation can override or confuse our instincts, leaving us disconnected from our inner guidance.

Rebuilding these instincts is like restoring an internal compass. Through practices such as mindfulness, somatic awareness, and intentional repetition, we can retrain the brain and body to recognize cues of safety and danger accurately. Over time, this process rewires our nervous system, strengthening trust in ourselves and bringing us back to a state of balance where our survival codes work for us rather than against us.

NOTES

....

....

....

....

....

....

....

....

....

....

....

SO HOW DO I BUILD THESE CODES BACK?

Bob Proctor, a Mentor of the Masses, recommends using your "Intuition," which is the key to survival and success.

Exercise: Start a 7-day 'Gut Check' diary. Write your first instinct in each moment before reacting. Start here.

_____

_____

_____

_____

_____

_____

_____

NOTES

··

··

··

··

··

··

··

··

··

··

··

Success Story

HERE COMES A SUCCESS STORY

INSERT YOUR PHOTO HERE

QUESTIONS?

infowisemarie@gmail.com

CHAPTER THREE

SITUATIONAL AWARENESS - READ A ROOM, SCAN A STREET

Are you on a walk? How often do you scan your surroundings? Do you wear one earbud? That's the best route. Are you leaving a Broadway Musical and scared of the predators that follow the attendees back to their rooms? Do you know if you walk inside the crowd, it works as a protective barrier? You jump out of it when you are near your destination. Call your Uber before waiting on the street.

Are you done shopping, and you are looking at your phone instead of your surroundings? Lock your vehicle as soon as you are in. Check your vehicle's backseat and trunk before entering. Take care of your business and leave the parking lot, especially during the holidays. Cover your packages with blankets and clothes, so the car looks messy vs. loaded with the goods. Always put the bags below window level for less of a view from afar.

Tip: Enter every room like it's a battlefield—exit plan, ally scan, tension check.

NOTES

....

....

....

....

....

....

....

....

....

....

....

CHECKLISTS

CHECK YOUR BOXES AS YOU SCAN THE ROOM

LOCATION

- ☐ Where are the exits?

- ☐ Are you seated facing the door?

- ☐ Is there a safe place your entire party knows and can get to?

PEOPLE

- ☐ Who is watching who?

- ☐ What is being unsaid, but is aparent through body language?

- ☐ What does your gut tell you about the people around you?

YOUR FAMILY

- ☐ Is your family protected?

- ☐ Do you have a process that the entire family knows in case one gets separated?

CHAPTER FOUR
CODES, CUES, & STREET SPEAK

USE YOUR INTUITION. AGGRESSION CAN BE FELT BEFORE IT IS SEEN.

Always watch people and see if they could be carrying weapons. Look for signs of the person packing, grabbing their back, waist, or ankle area. Look for knives in pockets that are hooked on or the shape of them in the pocket.

Phrase Bank: 'I'm good, fam', 'I hear you', 'Nah, I'll catch you later'

Exercise: Practice decoding body language in public (3 strangers/day).

NOTES

···

···

···

···

···

···

···

···

···

···

···

CHAPTER FIVE
RESOURCEFULNESS & QUICK-THINKING

 **Mini-Drill**

If your phone, cash, and ID were gone right now—what would you do?

_____

_____

_____

_____

_____

_____

_____

_____

WHAT YOU SHOULD DO

Contact your credit card companies by saving those numbers in your iCloud or Google account, so you can access them from another device.

Most states allow for duplicate IDs as long as they are not expired. Order it and always make photocopies of IDs and save them in the safe or in a place you can access.

Use your eyes, mouth, and ears as tools—ask, observe, adapt fast. Who is around, what are they doing, and who can you ask?

NOTES

....

....

....

....

....

....

....

....

....

....

....

Relationships TRUST

In your own words, what is trust?

_____

_____

_____

_____

List two things that can break trust:

1 _____   **2** _____

_____   _____

_____   _____

What practical things can you do to build trust?

_____

_____

_____

_____

Is teamwork possible without trust? Explain your answer:

_____

_____

_____

Who is someone you trust?

_____

_____

NOTES

....

....

....

....

....

....

....

....

....

....

....

My Go Bag

You should always have a go bag handy. You never Know when you will need to go at a moment's notice. This will allow you to grab and go as needed. It should include essentials and emergency funds.

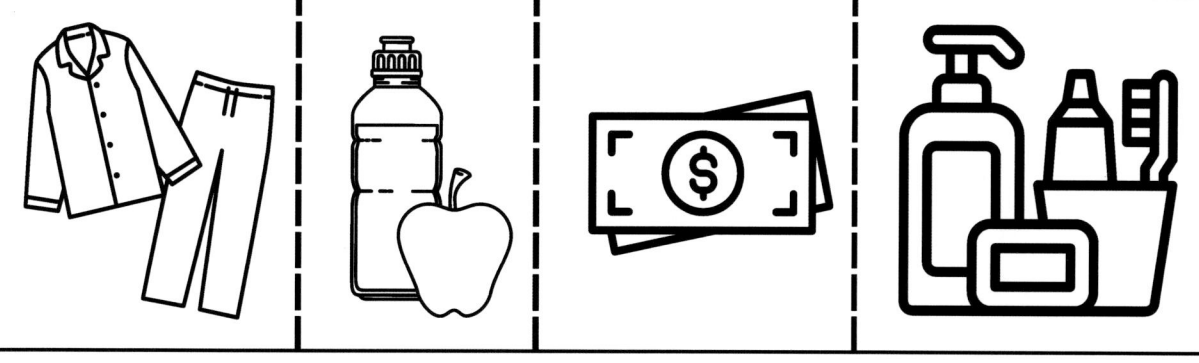

PACKING LIST
WHAT ARE YOU PACKING IN YOUR GO BAG?

NOTES

....

....

....

....

....

....

....

....

....

....

....

CHAPTER SIX
SURVIVAL PROTOCOLS

SHELTER

Trust your gut over a cheap deal. Seek visible, semi-secure public locations. Marie didn't stay in a shelter. She didn't feel safe in places like that. Use your intuition. Hustle and live in extended stay type accommodations. It's a place to have a clean bed, shower, kitchen, and TV for kids, along with safety and parking.

FOOD

Gas station bananas, convenience stores, cooking at transient locations, soup kitchens, and hygiene with wipes. Work on your health and fitness when funds are down for food. Walk everywhere, take the bus, and make smart choices like tuna and canned vegetables until you can obtain fresh sustenance.

Always trust your gut.

NOTES

....

....

....

....

....

....

....

....

....

....

....

CHAPTER SEVEN
PROTECTING YOUR ENERGY

Affirmation:

My peace is my power. No one gets to break it without my permission. No one takes my power unless I allow it.
No bully or sexual predator is going to win here. My mind, body, and soul are protected by my Higher Power and Spirit.

Boundary Drill:

Say 'No thanks' without explanation 5x/day.

"Hey, you should try this new skin cream."

No thanks.

NOTES

....

....

....

....

....

....

....

....

....

....

....

CHAPTER EIGHT
Pitfall Prevention

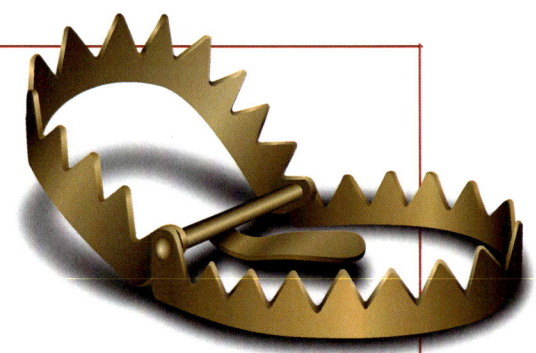

KNOW THE DIFFERENCE BETWEEN HUSTLERS WITH HEART AND PREDATORS WITH CHARM.

Red Flags: Fast promises, secrecy, guilt trips, and watch how they treat those close to them.

Some people lead with heart, lifting others up through honesty and genuine care. Others wear charm like a mask—smooth words hiding selfish motives. The difference reveals itself in the little things: rushed promises, shifting stories, subtle guilt trips, or how they treat those closest to them.

Pay attention to patterns, not just words. True character is shown in consistent actions, while deception eventually slips through the cracks.

NOTES

....

....

....

....

....

....

....

....

....

....

....

CHAPTER NINE
MIND OVER MAYHEM

POWER SONG OR PHRASE

What song or phrase can pull you back when slipping?

Grounding: 5 deep breaths, find one thing of each color, repeat mantra.

Remain calm. It is NOT the end of the world.

Take the time you need for yourself.

Walk, ponder, exercise, run, or drive safely to express your feelings positively.

NOTES

....

....

....

....

....

....

....

....

....

....

....

CHAPTER Ten

REINVENTION - YOUR COMEBACK PLAN

"You're not starting over. You're starting wiser."
– Natasha Brune

Goal   3 allies/programs = 1 bold step.

Enroll in a Mindset and Personal Development Immersion Course 1 + years

-This is for the rest of your life; you must study, follow the Laws of the Universe, and Surround Yourself with ONLY Elevated People..

-The past gangsters do not exist, unless they, too, have changed their lifestyle to be aligned with yours.

-Not everyone can remain connected, so it's important to evaluate yourself, your friendships, connections, and the like, all the time.

NOTES

....

....

....

....

....

....

....

....

....

....

....

CHAPTER ELEVEN

> ## SUBMIT TO COURT, FAMILY, OR STREET PRESSURE BY CHECKING INTO A RESIDENTIAL PROGRAM.

Rehab: It works if you work it, and it's true. Make that decision to get help regardless of what your situation is. ***Seek help***, and you will attract those to help you. Be flexible with whatever program you attend. Not all are the same, and if you can do research, Marie would select the hardest one available, like Habilitat, Inc., and/or DayTop Village in New York.

Jail: Turn yourself in. You'll immediately feel ten times better, and you can begin your new life.

Family: Work together to resolve internal and external issues. We get one life in this realm, make it count, and take care of ***YOU*** and ***YOUR family***, as long as it supports your goals.

Street: Get off the Street and check into rehab and/or a program to help you with what you are struggling with. Clear your name by the Street forgetting about you. Out of sight, out of mind.

NOTES

....

....

....

....

....

....

....

....

....

....

....

SIGNATURE COMMITMENT

MAKE THE DECISION
TO START TODAY

I _____ SURVIVED. NOW I RISE-
AND I WALK IN WISDOM.

Signed: _____

Date: _____

"You are the only problem you will ever have, and you are the only solution. Change is inevitable, personal growth is always a personal decision."
-Bob Proctor

MORE FROM NATASHA BRUNE

Titles By Natasha Brune
Wise Marie Adult Collection
Wise Marie East Coast Version, Volume 1
Real Estate Rabbit Hole Series (TBA) – Nonfiction
Adapted Screenplays Draft – Two Volumes of the Adult Books

The Wise Ladybug Series
Children and Young Adult Genre
Wise Marie, "Nugget From Heaven" (Released, published, being rewritten to YA)
Wise Ladybug, Tiny Houses and Bnbs (TBA)
Wise Ladybug, Upstate New York (TBA)
Wise Ladybug, Summer of 1978 (TBA)
Wise Ladybug, Summer of 1979 (TBA)
Wise Ladybug, Marie Goes Fishing (TBA)
Wise Ladybug, Jams, Jellies, Buttah and Milk (TBA)
Wise Ladybug, Greeks To Me & Tractors Rock (TBA)
Wise Ladybug, Aloha oe Anne (TBA)

Hawaii Stories

Wise Ladybug, Handprint Tans (TBA)
Wise Ladybug, I Am Strange Mom (TBA)
Wise Ladybug, No Animals Marie (TBA)
Wise Ladybug, Miss M's Art Class (TBA)
Wise Ladybug, Water Balloons & Washcloths (TBA)
Wise Ladybug, Peanut Butter Toast & Mochi (TBA)
Wise Ladybug, Mom Won A Trip to Hilo (TBA)
Wise Ladybug, Mom & The Chinese Beekeeper (TBA)
Wise Marie YA, A Country Club & Hawaiian Hot Dogs (TBA)
Wise Marie YA, Roller Skating & Suede (TBA)
Wise Marie YA, Jazz Dancing Will Cure You (TBA)

NOTES

....

....

....

....

....

....

....

....

....

....

....

NOTES

....

....

....

....

....

....

....

....

....

....

....

NOTES

....

....

....

....

....

....

....

....

....

....

....

NOTES

....

....

....

....

....

....

....

....

....

....

NOTES

....

....

....

....

....

....

....

....

....

....

....

Rights & Copyright Notice

WISE MARIE SURVIVAL WORKBOOK

STREET-LEVEL GUIDE TO LIFE MASTERY

The Wise Marie Survival Workbook is the hands-on companion to The Wise Marie Paradise Edition—a raw and transformative journey through resilience, intuition, and reinvention. Drawing from over a decade of lived experience, author Natasha Brune (aka Kimberly Cano) shares practical lessons for rebuilding instincts, protecting your energy, and mastering life from the ground up.

Through guided reflections, mindset drills, and street-smart strategies, this workbook invites readers to reconnect with their inner compass and rise above chaos with courage and clarity.

Whether you're healing from hardship, starting over, or learning to trust your intuition again—Wise Marie will meet you exactly where you are and show you how to begin again, wiser than before.

www.ingramcontent.com/pod-product-compliance
Lightning Source LLC
Chambersburg PA
CBRC090839120626
46551CB00008B/705